THANK You so much ★

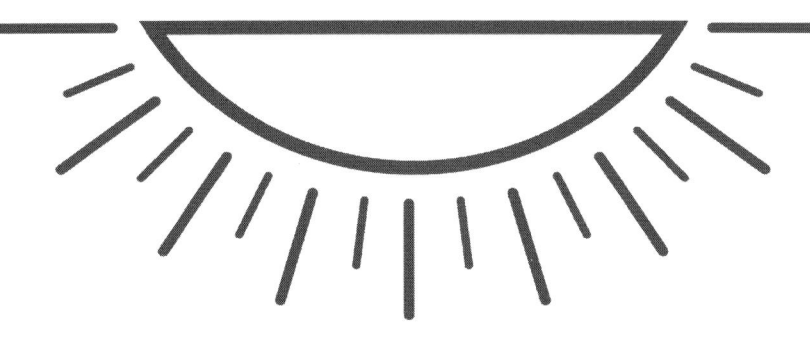

MORNING MEDITATION

DATE ___/___/___

TODAY'S FOCUS :

AN AFFIRMATION FOR TODAY :

WHAT I'GRATEFUL FOR :

WHAT I'M EXCITED ABOUT TODAY :

HOW I'LL MAKE SPACE FOR GRATITUDE TODAY :

MORNING MEDITATION

THINGS I DID TO MAKE A POSITIVE DIFFERENCE TODAY :

_____
_____
_____
_____

❏ HAPPY	❏ NEUTRAL	NOTES :
❏ CONTENT	❏ INSECURE	_____
❏ PROUD	❏ DISOURAGED	_____
❏ HOPEFUL	❏ DRAINED	_____
❏ LOVING	❏ SAD	_____
❏ CONNECTED	❏ SCARED	_____
❏ BALANCED	❏ ANGRY	_____
❏ JOYFUL	❏ ANNOYED	_____
❏ RELAXED	❏ STESSED	_____
❏ CREATIVE	❏ OVERWHELMED	
❏ EXCITED	❏ _____	
❏ _____		

A POSITIVE THOUGHT TO CARRY ME TO SLEEP

_____
_____
_____
_____

MORNING MEDITATION

DATE __/__/__

TODAY'S FOCUS :

AN AFFIRMATION FOR TODAY :

WHAT I' GRATEFUL FOR :

WHAT I'M EXCITED ABOUT TODAY :

HOW I'LL MAKE SPACE FOR GRATITUDE TODAY :

MORNING MEDITATION

THINGS I DID TO MAKE A POSITIVE DIFFERENCE TODAY :

_____
_____
_____
_____

❏ HAPPY	❏ NEUTRAL	NOTES :
❏ CONTENT	❏ INSECURE	_____
❏ PROUD	❏ DISOURAGED	_____
❏ HOPEFUL	❏ DRAINED	_____
❏ LOVING	❏ SAD	_____
❏ CONNECTED	❏ SCARED	_____
❏ BALANCED	❏ ANGRY	_____
❏ JOYFUL	❏ ANNOYED	_____
❏ RELAXED	❏ STESSED	_____
❏ CREATIVE	❏ OVERWHELMED	
❏ EXCITED	❏ _____	
❏ _____		

A POSITIVE THOUGHT TO CARRY ME TO SLEEP

_____
_____
_____
_____

MORNING MEDITATION

DATE __/__/__

TODAY'S FOCUS : _____

_____
_____
_____

AN AFFIRMATION FOR TODAY : _____

_____
_____
_____

WHAT I'GRATEFUL FOR : _____

_____
_____
_____

WHAT I'M EXCITED ABOUT TODAY : _____

_____
_____
_____

HOW I'LL MAKE SPACE FOR GRATITUDE TODAY : _____

_____
_____
_____

MORNING MEDITATION

THINGS I DID TO MAKE A POSITIVE DIFFERENCE TODAY :

_____
_____
_____
_____

❏ HAPPY	❏ NEUTRAL	NOTES :
❏ CONTENT	❏ INSECURE	_____
❏ PROUD	❏ DISOURAGED	_____
❏ HOPEFUL	❏ DRAINED	_____
❏ LOVING	❏ SAD	_____
❏ CONNECTED	❏ SCARED	_____
❏ BALANCED	❏ ANGRY	_____
❏ JOYFUL	❏ ANNOYED	_____
❏ RELAXED	❏ STESSED	_____
❏ CREATIVE	❏ OVERWHELMED	
❏ EXCITED	❏ _____	
❏ _____		

A POSITIVE THOUGHT TO CARRY ME TO SLEEP

_____
_____
_____
_____

MORNING MEDITATION

DATE __/__/__

TODAY'S FOCUS : _____

_____
_____
_____

AN AFFIRMATION FOR TODAY : _____

_____
_____
_____

WHAT I'GRATEFUL FOR : _____

_____
_____
_____

WHAT I'M EXCITED ABOUT TODAY : _____

_____
_____
_____

HOW I'LL MAKE SPACE FOR GRATITUDE TODAY : ___

_____
_____
_____

MORNING MEDITATION

THINGS I DID TO MAKE A POSITIVE DIFFERENCE TODAY :

_____
_____
_____
_____

❏ HAPPY	❏ NEUTRAL	NOTES :
❏ CONTENT	❏ INSECURE	_____
❏ PROUD	❏ DISOURAGED	_____
❏ HOPEFUL	❏ DRAINED	_____
❏ LOVING	❏ SAD	_____
❏ CONNECTED	❏ SCARED	_____
❏ BALANCED	❏ ANGRY	_____
❏ JOYFUL	❏ ANNOYED	_____
❏ RELAXED	❏ STESSED	_____
❏ CREATIVE	❏ OVERWHELMED	
❏ EXCITED	❏ _____	
❏ _____		

A POSITIVE THOUGHT TO CARRY ME TO SLEEP

_____
_____
_____
_____

With all my Thanks

MORNING MEDITATION

DATE ___/___/___

TODAY'S FOCUS :

AN AFFIRMATION FOR TODAY :

WHAT I'GRATEFUL FOR :

WHAT I'M EXCITED ABOUT TODAY :

HOW I'LL MAKE SPACE FOR GRATITUDE TODAY :

MORNING MEDITATION

THINGS I DID TO MAKE A POSITIVE DIFFERENCE TODAY :

_____
_____
_____

❏ HAPPY	❏ NEUTRAL	NOTES :
❏ CONTENT	❏ INSECURE	_____
❏ PROUD	❏ DISOURAGED	_____
❏ HOPEFUL	❏ DRAINED	_____
❏ LOVING	❏ SAD	_____
❏ CONNECTED	❏ SCARED	_____
❏ BALANCED	❏ ANGRY	_____
❏ JOYFUL	❏ ANNOYED	_____
❏ RELAXED	❏ STESSED	_____
❏ CREATIVE	❏ OVERWHELMED	
❏ EXCITED	❏ _____	
❏ _____		

A POSITIVE THOUGHT TO CARRY ME TO SLEEP

_____
_____
_____
_____

MORNING MEDITATION

DATE __/__/__

TODAY'S FOCUS :

AN AFFIRMATION FOR TODAY :

WHAT I'GRATEFUL FOR :

WHAT I'M EXCITED ABOUT TODAY :

HOW I'LL MAKE SPACE FOR GRATITUDE TODAY :

MORNING MEDITATION

THINGS I DID TO MAKE A POSITIVE DIFFERENCE TODAY :

_____
_____
_____
_____

❏ HAPPY	❏ NEUTRAL	NOTES :
❏ CONTENT	❏ INSECURE	_____
❏ PROUD	❏ DISOURAGED	_____
❏ HOPEFUL	❏ DRAINED	_____
❏ LOVING	❏ SAD	_____
❏ CONNECTED	❏ SCARED	_____
❏ BALANCED	❏ ANGRY	_____
❏ JOYFUL	❏ ANNOYED	_____
❏ RELAXED	❏ STESSED	_____
❏ CREATIVE	❏ OVERWHELMED	
❏ EXCITED	❏ _____	
❏ _____		

A POSITIVE THOUGHT TO CARRY ME TO SLEEP

_____
_____
_____
_____

MORNING MEDITATION

DATE ___/___/___

TODAY'S FOCUS : _____

AN AFFIRMATION FOR TODAY : _____

WHAT I'GRATEFUL FOR : _____

WHAT I'M EXCITED ABOUT TODAY : _____

HOW I'LL MAKE SPACE FOR GRATITUDE TODAY : _____

MORNING MEDITATION

THINGS I DID TO MAKE A POSITIVE DIFFERENCE TODAY :

_____
_____
_____
_____

❑ HAPPY   ❑ NEUTRAL   NOTES :
❑ CONTENT   ❑ INSECURE   _____
❑ PROUD   ❑ DISOURAGED   _____
❑ HOPEFUL   ❑ DRAINED   _____
❑ LOVING   ❑ SAD   _____
❑ CONNECTED   ❑ SCARED   _____
❑ BALANCED   ❑ ANGRY   _____
❑ JOYFUL   ❑ ANNOYED   _____
❑ RELAXED   ❑ STESSED   _____
❑ CREATIVE   ❑ OVERWHELMED
❑ EXCITED   ❑ _____
❑ _____

A POSITIVE THOUGHT TO CARRY ME TO SLEEP

_____
_____
_____
_____

MORNING MEDITATION

DATE __/__/__

TODAY'S FOCUS : _____

AN AFFIRMATION FOR TODAY : _____

WHAT I'GRATEFUL FOR : _____

WHAT I'M EXCITED ABOUT TODAY : _____

HOW I'LL MAKE SPACE FOR GRATITUDE TODAY : _____

MORNING MEDITATION

THINGS I DID TO MAKE A POSITIVE DIFFERENCE TODAY :

_____
_____
_____
_____

❏ HAPPY	❏ NEUTRAL	NOTES :
❏ CONTENT	❏ INSECURE	_____
❏ PROUD	❏ DISOURAGED	_____
❏ HOPEFUL	❏ DRAINED	_____
❏ LOVING	❏ SAD	_____
❏ CONNECTED	❏ SCARED	_____
❏ BALANCED	❏ ANGRY	_____
❏ JOYFUL	❏ ANNOYED	_____
❏ RELAXED	❏ STESSED	_____
❏ CREATIVE	❏ OVERWHELMED	
❏ EXCITED	❏ _____	
❏ _____		

A POSITIVE THOUGHT TO CARRY ME TO SLEEP

_____
_____
_____
_____

MORNING MEDITATION

DATE __/__/__

TODAY'S FOCUS : _____

AN AFFIRMATION FOR TODAY : _____

WHAT I'GRATEFUL FOR : _____

WHAT I'M EXCITED ABOUT TODAY : _____

HOW I'LL MAKE SPACE FOR GRATITUDE TODAY : _____

MORNING MEDITATION

THINGS I DID TO MAKE A POSITIVE DIFFERENCE TODAY :

_____
_____
_____
_____

❏ HAPPY	❏ NEUTRAL	NOTES :
❏ CONTENT	❏ INSECURE	_____
❏ PROUD	❏ DISOURAGED	_____
❏ HOPEFUL	❏ DRAINED	_____
❏ LOVING	❏ SAD	_____
❏ CONNECTED	❏ SCARED	_____
❏ BALANCED	❏ ANGRY	_____
❏ JOYFUL	❏ ANNOYED	_____
❏ RELAXED	❏ STESSED	_____
❏ CREATIVE	❏ OVERWHELMED	
❏ EXCITED	❏ _____	
❏ _____		

A POSITIVE THOUGHT TO CARRY ME TO SLEEP

_____
_____
_____
_____

Many Thanks

MORNING MEDITATION

DATE ___/___/___

TODAY'S FOCUS : _____

_____
_____
_____

AN AFFIRMATION FOR TODAY : _____

_____
_____
_____

WHAT I'GRATEFUL FOR : _____

_____
_____
_____

WHAT I'M EXCITED ABOUT TODAY : _____

_____
_____
_____

HOW I'LL MAKE SPACE FOR GRATITUDE TODAY : _____

_____
_____
_____

MORNING MEDITATION

THINGS I DID TO MAKE A POSITIVE DIFFERENCE TODAY :

_____
_____
_____
_____

❏ HAPPY	❏ NEUTRAL	NOTES :
❏ CONTENT	❏ INSECURE	_____
❏ PROUD	❏ DISOURAGED	_____
❏ HOPEFUL	❏ DRAINED	_____
❏ LOVING	❏ SAD	_____
❏ CONNECTED	❏ SCARED	_____
❏ BALANCED	❏ ANGRY	_____
❏ JOYFUL	❏ ANNOYED	_____
❏ RELAXED	❏ STESSED	_____
❏ CREATIVE	❏ OVERWHELMED	
❏ EXCITED	❏ _____	
❏ _____		

A POSITIVE THOUGHT TO CARRY ME TO SLEEP

_____
_____
_____
_____

MORNING MEDITATION

DATE ___/___/___

TODAY'S FOCUS :

AN AFFIRMATION FOR TODAY :

WHAT I'GRATEFUL FOR :

WHAT I'M EXCITED ABOUT TODAY :

HOW I'LL MAKE SPACE FOR GRATITUDE TODAY :

MORNING MEDITATION

THINGS I DID TO MAKE A POSITIVE DIFFERENCE TODAY :

_____
_____
_____
_____

- ❏ HAPPY
- ❏ CONTENT
- ❏ PROUD
- ❏ HOPEFUL
- ❏ LOVING
- ❏ CONNECTED
- ❏ BALANCED
- ❏ JOYFUL
- ❏ RELAXED
- ❏ CREATIVE
- ❏ EXCITED
- ❏ _____

- ❏ NEUTRAL
- ❏ INSECURE
- ❏ DISOURAGED
- ❏ DRAINED
- ❏ SAD
- ❏ SCARED
- ❏ ANGRY
- ❏ ANNOYED
- ❏ STESSED
- ❏ OVERWHELMED
- ❏ _____

NOTES :
_____
_____
_____
_____
_____
_____
_____

A POSITIVE THOUGHT TO CARRY ME TO SLEEP

_____
_____
_____
_____

MORNING MEDITATION

DATE ___/___/___

TODAY'S FOCUS : _____

_____
_____
_____

AN AFFIRMATION FOR TODAY : _____

_____
_____
_____

WHAT I' GRATEFUL FOR : _____

_____
_____
_____

WHAT I'M EXCITED ABOUT TODAY : _____

_____
_____
_____

HOW I'LL MAKE SPACE FOR GRATITUDE TODAY : _____

_____
_____
_____

MORNING MEDITATION

THINGS I DID TO MAKE A POSITIVE DIFFERENCE TODAY :

_____
_____
_____
_____

- ❏ HAPPY
- ❏ CONTENT
- ❏ PROUD
- ❏ HOPEFUL
- ❏ LOVING
- ❏ CONNECTED
- ❏ BALANCED
- ❏ JOYFUL
- ❏ RELAXED
- ❏ CREATIVE
- ❏ EXCITED
- ❏ _____

- ❏ NEUTRAL
- ❏ INSECURE
- ❏ DISOURAGED
- ❏ DRAINED
- ❏ SAD
- ❏ SCARED
- ❏ ANGRY
- ❏ ANNOYED
- ❏ STESSED
- ❏ OVERWHELMED
- ❏ _____

NOTES :
_____
_____
_____
_____
_____
_____
_____

A POSITIVE THOUGHT TO CARRY ME TO SLEEP

_____
_____
_____
_____

MORNING MEDITATION

DATE ___/___/___

TODAY'S FOCUS :

AN AFFIRMATION FOR TODAY :

WHAT I'GRATEFUL FOR :

WHAT I'M EXCITED ABOUT TODAY :

HOW I'LL MAKE SPACE FOR GRATITUDE TODAY :

MORNING MEDITATION

THINGS I DID TO MAKE A POSITIVE DIFFERENCE TODAY :

_____
_____
_____
_____

❑ HAPPY	❑ NEUTRAL	NOTES :
❑ CONTENT	❑ INSECURE	_____
❑ PROUD	❑ DISOURAGED	_____
❑ HOPEFUL	❑ DRAINED	_____
❑ LOVING	❑ SAD	_____
❑ CONNECTED	❑ SCARED	_____
❑ BALANCED	❑ ANGRY	_____
❑ JOYFUL	❑ ANNOYED	_____
❑ RELAXED	❑ STESSED	_____
❑ CREATIVE	❑ OVERWHELMED	
❑ EXCITED	❑ _____	
❑ _____		

A POSITIVE THOUGHT TO CARRY ME TO SLEEP

_____
_____
_____
_____

THANK You so much ★

MORNING MEDITATION

DATE __/__/__

TODAY'S FOCUS : _____

AN AFFIRMATION FOR TODAY : _____

WHAT I'GRATEFUL FOR : _____

WHAT I'M EXCITED ABOUT TODAY : _____

HOW I'LL MAKE SPACE FOR GRATITUDE TODAY : _____

MORNING MEDITATION

THINGS I DID TO MAKE A POSITIVE DIFFERENCE TODAY :

_____

_____

_____

_____

❏ HAPPY	❏ NEUTRAL	NOTES :
❏ CONTENT	❏ INSECURE	_____
❏ PROUD	❏ DISOURAGED	_____
❏ HOPEFUL	❏ DRAINED	_____
❏ LOVING	❏ SAD	_____
❏ CONNECTED	❏ SCARED	_____
❏ BALANCED	❏ ANGRY	_____
❏ JOYFUL	❏ ANNOYED	_____
❏ RELAXED	❏ STESSED	_____
❏ CREATIVE	❏ OVERWHELMED	
❏ EXCITED	❏ _____	
❏ _____		

A POSITIVE THOUGHT TO CARRY ME TO SLEEP

_____

_____

_____

_____

MORNING MEDITATION

DATE ___/___/___

TODAY'S FOCUS :

AN AFFIRMATION FOR TODAY :

WHAT I'GRATEFUL FOR :

WHAT I'M EXCITED ABOUT TODAY :

HOW I'LL MAKE SPACE FOR GRATITUDE TODAY :

MORNING MEDITATION

THINGS I DID TO MAKE A POSITIVE DIFFERENCE TODAY :

_____

_____

_____

_____

❏ HAPPY	❏ NEUTRAL	NOTES :
❏ CONTENT	❏ INSECURE	_____
❏ PROUD	❏ DISOURAGED	_____
❏ HOPEFUL	❏ DRAINED	_____
❏ LOVING	❏ SAD	_____
❏ CONNECTED	❏ SCARED	_____
❏ BALANCED	❏ ANGRY	_____
❏ JOYFUL	❏ ANNOYED	_____
❏ RELAXED	❏ STESSED	_____
❏ CREATIVE	❏ OVERWHELMED	
❏ EXCITED	❏ _____	
❏ _____		

A POSITIVE THOUGHT TO CARRY ME TO SLEEP

_____

_____

_____

_____

MORNING MEDITATION

DATE ___/___/___

TODAY'S FOCUS : _____

_____
_____
_____

AN AFFIRMATION FOR TODAY : _____

_____
_____
_____

WHAT I'GRATEFUL FOR : _____

_____
_____
_____

WHAT I'M EXCITED ABOUT TODAY : _____

_____
_____
_____

HOW I'LL MAKE SPACE FOR GRATITUDE TODAY : _____

_____
_____
_____

MORNING MEDITATION

THINGS I DID TO MAKE A POSITIVE DIFFERENCE TODAY :

_____
_____
_____
_____

❏ HAPPY	❏ NEUTRAL	NOTES :
❏ CONTENT	❏ INSECURE	_____
❏ PROUD	❏ DISOURAGED	_____
❏ HOPEFUL	❏ DRAINED	_____
❏ LOVING	❏ SAD	_____
❏ CONNECTED	❏ SCARED	_____
❏ BALANCED	❏ ANGRY	_____
❏ JOYFUL	❏ ANNOYED	_____
❏ RELAXED	❏ STESSED	_____
❏ CREATIVE	❏ OVERWHELMED	
❏ EXCITED	❏ _____	
❏ _____		

A POSITIVE THOUGHT TO CARRY ME TO SLEEP

_____
_____
_____
_____
_____

MORNING MEDITATION

DATE __/__/__

TODAY'S FOCUS : _____

_____
_____
_____

AN AFFIRMATION FOR TODAY : _____

_____
_____
_____

WHAT I'GRATEFUL FOR : _____

_____
_____
_____

WHAT I'M EXCITED ABOUT TODAY : _____

_____
_____
_____
_____

HOW I'LL MAKE SPACE FOR GRATITUDE TODAY : _____

_____
_____
_____
_____

MORNING MEDITATION

THINGS I DID TO MAKE A POSITIVE DIFFERENCE TODAY :

_____
_____
_____
_____

❏ HAPPY	❏ NEUTRAL	NOTES :
❏ CONTENT	❏ INSECURE	_____
❏ PROUD	❏ DISOURAGED	_____
❏ HOPEFUL	❏ DRAINED	_____
❏ LOVING	❏ SAD	_____
❏ CONNECTED	❏ SCARED	_____
❏ BALANCED	❏ ANGRY	_____
❏ JOYFUL	❏ ANNOYED	_____
❏ RELAXED	❏ STESSED	_____
❏ CREATIVE	❏ OVERWHELMED	
❏ EXCITED	❏ _____	
❏ _____		

A POSITIVE THOUGHT TO CARRY ME TO SLEEP

_____
_____
_____
_____

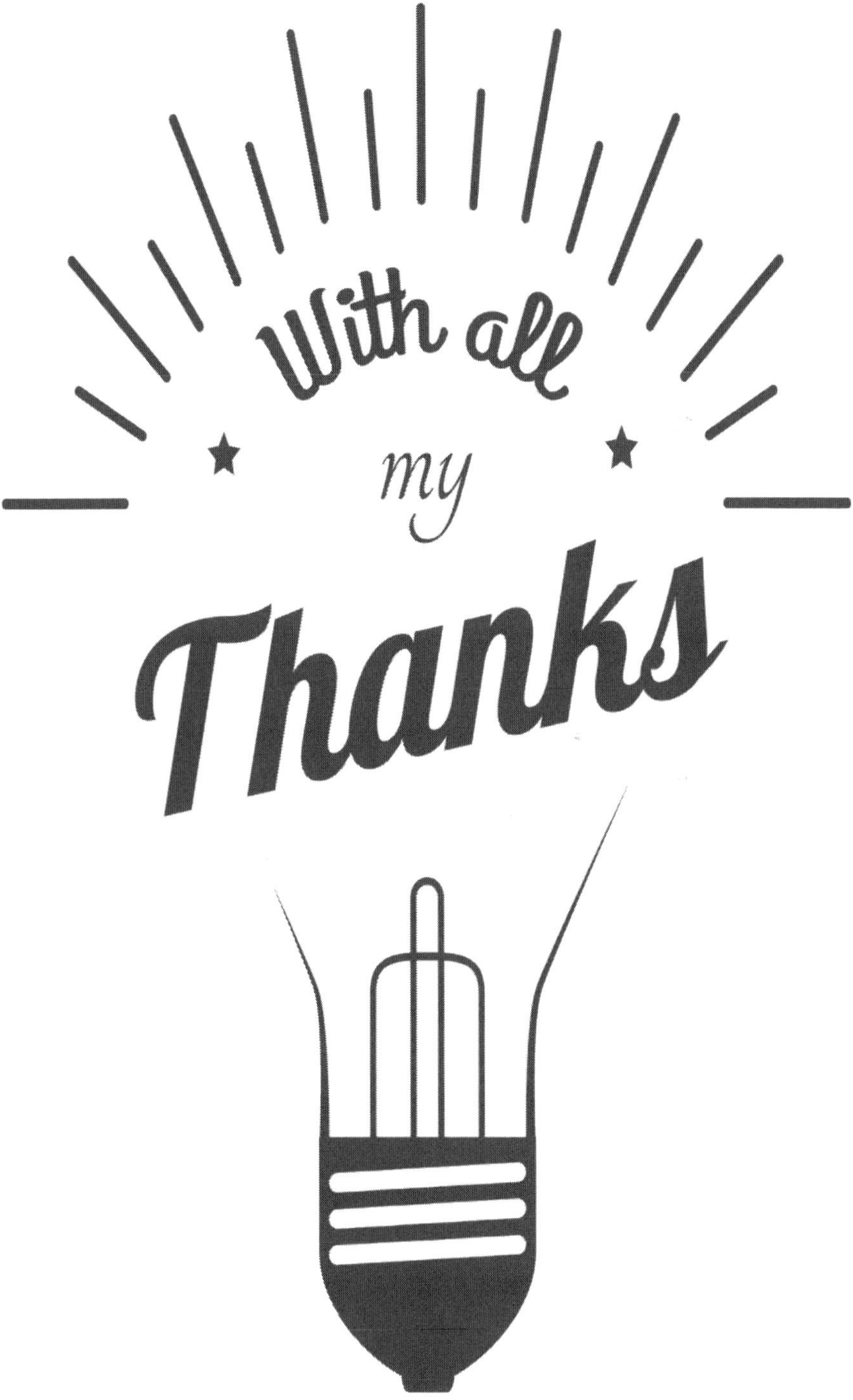
With all
my
Thanks

MORNING MEDITATION

DATE __/__/__

TODAY'S FOCUS : _____

_____
_____
_____

AN AFFIRMATION FOR TODAY : _____

_____
_____
_____

WHAT I'GRATEFUL FOR : _____

_____
_____
_____

WHAT I'M EXCITED ABOUT TODAY : _____

_____
_____
_____

HOW I'LL MAKE SPACE FOR GRATITUDE TODAY : _____

_____
_____
_____

MORNING MEDITATION

THINGS I DID TO MAKE A POSITIVE DIFFERENCE TODAY :

_____
_____
_____
_____

❑ HAPPY	❑ NEUTRAL	NOTES :
❑ CONTENT	❑ INSECURE	_____
❑ PROUD	❑ DISOURAGED	_____
❑ HOPEFUL	❑ DRAINED	_____
❑ LOVING	❑ SAD	_____
❑ CONNECTED	❑ SCARED	_____
❑ BALANCED	❑ ANGRY	_____
❑ JOYFUL	❑ ANNOYED	_____
❑ RELAXED	❑ STESSED	_____
❑ CREATIVE	❑ OVERWHELMED	
❑ EXCITED	❑ _____	
❑ _____		

A POSITIVE THOUGHT TO CARRY ME TO SLEEP

_____
_____
_____
_____

MORNING MEDITATION

DATE ___/___/___

TODAY'S FOCUS : _____

_____
_____
_____

AN AFFIRMATION FOR TODAY : _____

_____
_____
_____

WHAT I'GRATEFUL FOR : _____

_____
_____
_____

WHAT I'M EXCITED ABOUT TODAY : _____

_____
_____
_____

HOW I'LL MAKE SPACE FOR GRATITUDE TODAY : _____

_____
_____
_____

MORNING MEDITATION

THINGS I DID TO MAKE A POSITIVE DIFFERENCE TODAY :

_____
_____
_____
_____

❏ HAPPY	❏ NEUTRAL	NOTES :
❏ CONTENT	❏ INSECURE	_____
❏ PROUD	❏ DISOURAGED	_____
❏ HOPEFUL	❏ DRAINED	_____
❏ LOVING	❏ SAD	_____
❏ CONNECTED	❏ SCARED	_____
❏ BALANCED	❏ ANGRY	_____
❏ JOYFUL	❏ ANNOYED	_____
❏ RELAXED	❏ STESSED	_____
❏ CREATIVE	❏ OVERWHELMED	
❏ EXCITED	❏ _____	
❏ _____		

A POSITIVE THOUGHT TO CARRY ME TO SLEEP

_____
_____
_____
_____

MORNING MEDITATION

DATE ___/___/___

TODAY'S FOCUS :

AN AFFIRMATION FOR TODAY :

WHAT I'GRATEFUL FOR :

WHAT I'M EXCITED ABOUT TODAY :

HOW I'LL MAKE SPACE FOR GRATITUDE TODAY :

MORNING MEDITATION

THINGS I DID TO MAKE A POSITIVE DIFFERENCE TODAY :

_____
_____
_____
_____

❏ HAPPY	❏ NEUTRAL	NOTES :
❏ CONTENT	❏ INSECURE	_____
❏ PROUD	❏ DISOURAGED	_____
❏ HOPEFUL	❏ DRAINED	_____
❏ LOVING	❏ SAD	_____
❏ CONNECTED	❏ SCARED	_____
❏ BALANCED	❏ ANGRY	_____
❏ JOYFUL	❏ ANNOYED	_____
❏ RELAXED	❏ STESSED	_____
❏ CREATIVE	❏ OVERWHELMED	
❏ EXCITED	❏ _____	
❏ _____		

A POSITIVE THOUGHT TO CARRY ME TO SLEEP

_____
_____
_____
_____

MORNING MEDITATION

DATE ___/___/___

TODAY'S FOCUS : _____

AN AFFIRMATION FOR TODAY : _____

WHAT I'GRATEFUL FOR : _____

WHAT I'M EXCITED ABOUT TODAY : _____

HOW I'LL MAKE SPACE FOR GRATITUDE TODAY : _____

MORNING MEDITATION

THINGS I DID TO MAKE A POSITIVE DIFFERENCE TODAY :

_____
_____
_____
_____

- ❏ HAPPY
- ❏ CONTENT
- ❏ PROUD
- ❏ HOPEFUL
- ❏ LOVING
- ❏ CONNECTED
- ❏ BALANCED
- ❏ JOYFUL
- ❏ RELAXED
- ❏ CREATIVE
- ❏ EXCITED
- ❏ _____

- ❏ NEUTRAL
- ❏ INSECURE
- ❏ DISOURAGED
- ❏ DRAINED
- ❏ SAD
- ❏ SCARED
- ❏ ANGRY
- ❏ ANNOYED
- ❏ STESSED
- ❏ OVERWHELMED
- ❏ _____

NOTES :

_____
_____
_____
_____
_____
_____
_____
_____
_____

A POSITIVE THOUGHT TO CARRY ME TO SLEEP

_____
_____
_____
_____

With all my Thanks

MORNING MEDITATION

DATE __/__/__

TODAY'S FOCUS : _____

_____
_____
_____

AN AFFIRMATION FOR TODAY : _____

_____
_____
_____

WHAT I'GRATEFUL FOR : _____

_____
_____
_____

WHAT I'M EXCITED ABOUT TODAY : _____

_____
_____
_____

HOW I'LL MAKE SPACE FOR GRATITUDE TODAY : _____

_____
_____
_____

MORNING MEDITATION

THINGS I DID TO MAKE A POSITIVE DIFFERENCE TODAY :

_____
_____
_____

❏ HAPPY	❏ NEUTRAL	NOTES :
❏ CONTENT	❏ INSECURE	_____
❏ PROUD	❏ DISOURAGED	_____
❏ HOPEFUL	❏ DRAINED	_____
❏ LOVING	❏ SAD	_____
❏ CONNECTED	❏ SCARED	_____
❏ BALANCED	❏ ANGRY	_____
❏ JOYFUL	❏ ANNOYED	_____
❏ RELAXED	❏ STESSED	_____
❏ CREATIVE	❏ OVERWHELMED	
❏ EXCITED	❏ _____	
❏ _____		

A POSITIVE THOUGHT TO CARRY ME TO SLEEP

_____
_____
_____
_____

Many Thanks

MORNING MEDITATION

DATE ___/___/___

TODAY'S FOCUS : _____

_____

_____

_____

AN AFFIRMATION FOR TODAY : _____

_____

_____

WHAT I'GRATEFUL FOR : _____

_____

_____

WHAT I'M EXCITED ABOUT TODAY : _____

_____

_____

_____

HOW I'LL MAKE SPACE FOR GRATITUDE TODAY : _____

_____

_____

MORNING MEDITATION

THINGS I DID TO MAKE A POSITIVE DIFFERENCE TODAY :

_____

_____

_____

_____

- ❏ HAPPY
- ❏ CONTENT
- ❏ PROUD
- ❏ HOPEFUL
- ❏ LOVING
- ❏ CONNECTED
- ❏ BALANCED
- ❏ JOYFUL
- ❏ RELAXED
- ❏ CREATIVE
- ❏ EXCITED
- ❏ _____

- ❏ NEUTRAL
- ❏ INSECURE
- ❏ DISOURAGED
- ❏ DRAINED
- ❏ SAD
- ❏ SCARED
- ❏ ANGRY
- ❏ ANNOYED
- ❏ STESSED
- ❏ OVERWHELMED
- ❏ _____

NOTES :

_____
_____
_____
_____
_____
_____
_____

A POSITIVE THOUGHT TO CARRY ME TO SLEEP

_____

_____

_____

_____

MORNING MEDITATION

DATE ___/___/___

TODAY'S FOCUS :

AN AFFIRMATION FOR TODAY :

WHAT I'GRATEFUL FOR :

WHAT I'M EXCITED ABOUT TODAY :

HOW I'LL MAKE SPACE FOR GRATITUDE TODAY :

MORNING MEDITATION

THINGS I DID TO MAKE A POSITIVE DIFFERENCE TODAY :

_____
_____
_____
_____

❏ HAPPY	❏ NEUTRAL	NOTES :
❏ CONTENT	❏ INSECURE	_____
❏ PROUD	❏ DISOURAGED	_____
❏ HOPEFUL	❏ DRAINED	_____
❏ LOVING	❏ SAD	_____
❏ CONNECTED	❏ SCARED	_____
❏ BALANCED	❏ ANGRY	_____
❏ JOYFUL	❏ ANNOYED	_____
❏ RELAXED	❏ STESSED	_____
❏ CREATIVE	❏ OVERWHELMED	
❏ EXCITED	❏ _____	
❏ _____		

A POSITIVE THOUGHT TO CARRY ME TO SLEEP

_____
_____
_____
_____

MORNING MEDITATION

DATE __/__/__

TODAY'S FOCUS : _____

_____

_____

_____

AN AFFIRMATION FOR TODAY : _____

_____

_____

_____

WHAT I'GRATEFUL FOR : _____

_____

_____

_____

WHAT I'M EXCITED ABOUT TODAY : _____

_____

_____

_____

HOW I'LL MAKE SPACE FOR GRATITUDE TODAY : ____

_____

_____

_____

MORNING MEDITATION

THINGS I DID TO MAKE A POSITIVE DIFFERENCE TODAY :

_____
_____
_____

❏ HAPPY	❏ NEUTRAL	NOTES :
❏ CONTENT	❏ INSECURE	_____
❏ PROUD	❏ DISOURAGED	_____
❏ HOPEFUL	❏ DRAINED	_____
❏ LOVING	❏ SAD	_____
❏ CONNECTED	❏ SCARED	_____
❏ BALANCED	❏ ANGRY	_____
❏ JOYFUL	❏ ANNOYED	_____
❏ RELAXED	❏ STESSED	_____
❏ CREATIVE	❏ OVERWHELMED	
❏ EXCITED	❏ _____	
❏ _____		

A POSITIVE THOUGHT TO CARRY ME TO SLEEP

_____
_____
_____
_____

MORNING MEDITATION

DATE ___/___/___

TODAY'S FOCUS :

AN AFFIRMATION FOR TODAY :

WHAT I'GRATEFUL FOR :

WHAT I'M EXCITED ABOUT TODAY :

HOW I'LL MAKE SPACE FOR GRATITUDE TODAY :

MORNING MEDITATION

THINGS I DID TO MAKE A POSITIVE DIFFERENCE TODAY :

_____
_____
_____
_____

❏ HAPPY	❏ NEUTRAL	NOTES :
❏ CONTENT	❏ INSECURE	_____
❏ PROUD	❏ DISOURAGED	_____
❏ HOPEFUL	❏ DRAINED	_____
❏ LOVING	❏ SAD	_____
❏ CONNECTED	❏ SCARED	_____
❏ BALANCED	❏ ANGRY	_____
❏ JOYFUL	❏ ANNOYED	_____
❏ RELAXED	❏ STESSED	_____
❏ CREATIVE	❏ OVERWHELMED	
❏ EXCITED	❏ _____	
❏ _____		

A POSITIVE THOUGHT TO CARRY ME TO SLEEP

_____
_____
_____
_____

THANK You so much ★

MORNING MEDITATION

DATE ___/___/___

TODAY'S FOCUS : _____

_____
_____
_____

AN AFFIRMATION FOR TODAY : _____

_____
_____
_____

WHAT I'GRATEFUL FOR : _____

_____
_____
_____

WHAT I'M EXCITED ABOUT TODAY : _____

_____
_____
_____
_____

HOW I'LL MAKE SPACE FOR GRATITUDE TODAY : _____

_____
_____
_____
_____

MORNING MEDITATION

THINGS I DID TO MAKE A POSITIVE DIFFERENCE TODAY :

_____
_____
_____

❏ HAPPY	❏ NEUTRAL	NOTES :
❏ CONTENT	❏ INSECURE	_____
❏ PROUD	❏ DISOURAGED	_____
❏ HOPEFUL	❏ DRAINED	_____
❏ LOVING	❏ SAD	_____
❏ CONNECTED	❏ SCARED	_____
❏ BALANCED	❏ ANGRY	_____
❏ JOYFUL	❏ ANNOYED	_____
❏ RELAXED	❏ STESSED	_____
❏ CREATIVE	❏ OVERWHELMED	
❏ EXCITED	❏ _____	
❏ _____		

A POSITIVE THOUGHT TO CARRY ME TO SLEEP

_____
_____
_____
_____

MORNING MEDITATION

DATE ___/___/___

TODAY'S FOCUS : _____

AN AFFIRMATION FOR TODAY : _____

WHAT I'GRATEFUL FOR : _____

WHAT I'M EXCITED ABOUT TODAY : _____

HOW I'LL MAKE SPACE FOR GRATITUDE TODAY : _____

MORNING MEDITATION

THINGS I DID TO MAKE A POSITIVE DIFFERENCE TODAY :

_____
_____
_____

- ❏ HAPPY
- ❏ CONTENT
- ❏ PROUD
- ❏ HOPEFUL
- ❏ LOVING
- ❏ CONNECTED
- ❏ BALANCED
- ❏ JOYFUL
- ❏ RELAXED
- ❏ CREATIVE
- ❏ EXCITED
- ❏ _____

- ❏ NEUTRAL
- ❏ INSECURE
- ❏ DISOURAGED
- ❏ DRAINED
- ❏ SAD
- ❏ SCARED
- ❏ ANGRY
- ❏ ANNOYED
- ❏ STESSED
- ❏ OVERWHELMED
- ❏ _____

NOTES :
_____
_____
_____
_____
_____
_____
_____
_____

A POSITIVE THOUGHT TO CARRY ME TO SLEEP

_____
_____
_____
_____

MORNING MEDITATION

DATE ___ / ___ / ___

TODAY'S FOCUS : _____

_____

_____

_____

AN AFFIRMATION FOR TODAY : _____

_____

_____

_____

WHAT I'GRATEFUL FOR : _____

_____

_____

_____

WHAT I'M EXCITED ABOUT TODAY : _____

_____

_____

_____

HOW I'LL MAKE SPACE FOR GRATITUDE TODAY : _____

_____

_____

_____

MORNING MEDITATION

THINGS I DID TO MAKE A POSITIVE DIFFERENCE TODAY :

_____
_____

❏ HAPPY	❏ NEUTRAL	NOTES :
❏ CONTENT	❏ INSECURE	_____
❏ PROUD	❏ DISOURAGED	_____
❏ HOPEFUL	❏ DRAINED	_____
❏ LOVING	❏ SAD	_____
❏ CONNECTED	❏ SCARED	_____
❏ BALANCED	❏ ANGRY	_____
❏ JOYFUL	❏ ANNOYED	_____
❏ RELAXED	❏ STESSED	_____
❏ CREATIVE	❏ OVERWHELMED	
❏ EXCITED	❏ _____	
❏ _____		

A POSITIVE THOUGHT TO CARRY ME TO SLEEP

_____
_____
_____
_____

MORNING MEDITATION

DATE ___/___/___

TODAY'S FOCUS :

AN AFFIRMATION FOR TODAY :

WHAT I'GRATEFUL FOR :

WHAT I'M EXCITED ABOUT TODAY :

HOW I'LL MAKE SPACE FOR GRATITUDE TODAY :

MORNING MEDITATION

THINGS I DID TO MAKE A POSITIVE DIFFERENCE TODAY :

_____
_____
_____

❏ HAPPY	❏ NEUTRAL	NOTES :
❏ CONTENT	❏ INSECURE	_____
❏ PROUD	❏ DISOURAGED	_____
❏ HOPEFUL	❏ DRAINED	_____
❏ LOVING	❏ SAD	_____
❏ CONNECTED	❏ SCARED	_____
❏ BALANCED	❏ ANGRY	_____
❏ JOYFUL	❏ ANNOYED	_____
❏ RELAXED	❏ STESSED	_____
❏ CREATIVE	❏ OVERWHELMED	
❏ EXCITED	❏ _____	
❏ _____		

A POSITIVE THOUGHT TO CARRY ME TO SLEEP

_____
_____
_____
_____

With all my Thanks

MORNING MEDITATION

DATE ___/___/___

TODAY'S FOCUS :

AN AFFIRMATION FOR TODAY :

WHAT I'GRATEFUL FOR :

WHAT I'M EXCITED ABOUT TODAY :

HOW I'LL MAKE SPACE FOR GRATITUDE TODAY :

MORNING MEDITATION

THINGS I DID TO MAKE A POSITIVE DIFFERENCE TODAY :

_____
_____
_____
_____

		NOTES :
❏ HAPPY	❏ NEUTRAL	
❏ CONTENT	❏ INSECURE	_____
❏ PROUD	❏ DISOURAGED	_____
❏ HOPEFUL	❏ DRAINED	_____
❏ LOVING	❏ SAD	_____
❏ CONNECTED	❏ SCARED	_____
❏ BALANCED	❏ ANGRY	_____
❏ JOYFUL	❏ ANNOYED	_____
❏ RELAXED	❏ STESSED	_____
❏ CREATIVE	❏ OVERWHELMED	
❏ EXCITED	❏ _____	
❏ _____		

A POSITIVE THOUGHT TO CARRY ME TO SLEEP

_____
_____
_____
_____

MORNING MEDITATION

DATE __/__/__

TODAY'S FOCUS :

AN AFFIRMATION FOR TODAY :

WHAT I'GRATEFUL FOR :

WHAT I'M EXCITED ABOUT TODAY :

HOW I'LL MAKE SPACE FOR GRATITUDE TODAY :

MORNING MEDITATION

THINGS I DID TO MAKE A POSITIVE DIFFERENCE TODAY :

_____
_____
_____

❏ HAPPY	❏ NEUTRAL	NOTES :
❏ CONTENT	❏ INSECURE	_____
❏ PROUD	❏ DISOURAGED	_____
❏ HOPEFUL	❏ DRAINED	_____
❏ LOVING	❏ SAD	_____
❏ CONNECTED	❏ SCARED	_____
❏ BALANCED	❏ ANGRY	_____
❏ JOYFUL	❏ ANNOYED	_____
❏ RELAXED	❏ STESSED	_____
❏ CREATIVE	❏ OVERWHELMED	
❏ EXCITED	❏ _____	
❏ _____		

A POSITIVE THOUGHT TO CARRY ME TO SLEEP

_____
_____
_____
_____

MORNING MEDITATION

DATE ___/___/___

TODAY'S FOCUS : _____

AN AFFIRMATION FOR TODAY : _____

WHAT I'GRATEFUL FOR : _____

WHAT I'M EXCITED ABOUT TODAY : _____

HOW I'LL MAKE SPACE FOR GRATITUDE TODAY : _____

MORNING MEDITATION

THINGS I DID TO MAKE A POSITIVE DIFFERENCE TODAY :

- ❏ HAPPY
- ❏ CONTENT
- ❏ PROUD
- ❏ HOPEFUL
- ❏ LOVING
- ❏ CONNECTED
- ❏ BALANCED
- ❏ JOYFUL
- ❏ RELAXED
- ❏ CREATIVE
- ❏ EXCITED
- ❏ _____

- ❏ NEUTRAL
- ❏ INSECURE
- ❏ DISOURAGED
- ❏ DRAINED
- ❏ SAD
- ❏ SCARED
- ❏ ANGRY
- ❏ ANNOYED
- ❏ STESSED
- ❏ OVERWHELMED
- ❏ _____

NOTES :

A POSITIVE THOUGHT TO CARRY ME TO SLEEP

MORNING MEDITATION

DATE ___/___/___

TODAY'S FOCUS : _____

AN AFFIRMATION FOR TODAY : _____

WHAT I'GRATEFUL FOR : _____

WHAT I'M EXCITED ABOUT TODAY : _____

HOW I'LL MAKE SPACE FOR GRATITUDE TODAY : _____

MORNING MEDITATION

THINGS I DID TO MAKE A POSITIVE DIFFERENCE TODAY :

- ❏ HAPPY
- ❏ CONTENT
- ❏ PROUD
- ❏ HOPEFUL
- ❏ LOVING
- ❏ CONNECTED
- ❏ BALANCED
- ❏ JOYFUL
- ❏ RELAXED
- ❏ CREATIVE
- ❏ EXCITED
- ❏ _____

- ❏ NEUTRAL
- ❏ INSECURE
- ❏ DISOURAGED
- ❏ DRAINED
- ❏ SAD
- ❏ SCARED
- ❏ ANGRY
- ❏ ANNOYED
- ❏ STESSED
- ❏ OVERWHELMED
- ❏ _____

NOTES :

A POSITIVE THOUGHT TO CARRY ME TO SLEEP

MORNING MEDITATION

DATE __/__/__

TODAY'S FOCUS : _____

AN AFFIRMATION FOR TODAY : _____

WHAT I'GRATEFUL FOR : _____

WHAT I'M EXCITED ABOUT TODAY : _____

HOW I'LL MAKE SPACE FOR GRATITUDE TODAY : _____

MORNING MEDITATION

THINGS I DID TO MAKE A POSITIVE DIFFERENCE TODAY :

_____
_____
_____
_____

❏ HAPPY	❏ NEUTRAL	NOTES :
❏ CONTENT	❏ INSECURE	_____
❏ PROUD	❏ DISOURAGED	_____
❏ HOPEFUL	❏ DRAINED	_____
❏ LOVING	❏ SAD	_____
❏ CONNECTED	❏ SCARED	_____
❏ BALANCED	❏ ANGRY	_____
❏ JOYFUL	❏ ANNOYED	_____
❏ RELAXED	❏ STESSED	_____
❏ CREATIVE	❏ OVERWHELMED	
❏ EXCITED	❏ _____	
❏ _____		

A POSITIVE THOUGHT TO CARRY ME TO SLEEP

_____
_____
_____
_____

Many Thanks

MORNING MEDITATION

DATE ___/___/___

TODAY'S FOCUS : _____

AN AFFIRMATION FOR TODAY : _____

WHAT I'GRATEFUL FOR : _____

WHAT I'M EXCITED ABOUT TODAY : _____

HOW I'LL MAKE SPACE FOR GRATITUDE TODAY : _____

MORNING MEDITATION

THINGS I DID TO MAKE A POSITIVE DIFFERENCE TODAY :

_____

_____

_____

		NOTES :
❏ HAPPY	❏ NEUTRAL	
❏ CONTENT	❏ INSECURE	_____
❏ PROUD	❏ DISOURAGED	_____
❏ HOPEFUL	❏ DRAINED	_____
❏ LOVING	❏ SAD	_____
❏ CONNECTED	❏ SCARED	_____
❏ BALANCED	❏ ANGRY	
❏ JOYFUL	❏ ANNOYED	_____
❏ RELAXED	❏ STESSED	_____
❏ CREATIVE	❏ OVERWHELMED	
❏ EXCITED	❏ _____	
❏ _____		

A POSITIVE THOUGHT TO CARRY ME TO SLEEP

_____

_____

_____

_____

MORNING MEDITATION

DATE __/__/__

TODAY'S FOCUS :

AN AFFIRMATION FOR TODAY :

WHAT I'GRATEFUL FOR :

WHAT I'M EXCITED ABOUT TODAY :

HOW I'LL MAKE SPACE FOR GRATITUDE TODAY :

MORNING MEDITATION

THINGS I DID TO MAKE A POSITIVE DIFFERENCE TODAY :

_____
_____
_____

❏ HAPPY	❏ NEUTRAL	NOTES :
❏ CONTENT	❏ INSECURE	_____
❏ PROUD	❏ DISOURAGED	_____
❏ HOPEFUL	❏ DRAINED	_____
❏ LOVING	❏ SAD	_____
❏ CONNECTED	❏ SCARED	_____
❏ BALANCED	❏ ANGRY	_____
❏ JOYFUL	❏ ANNOYED	_____
❏ RELAXED	❏ STESSED	_____
❏ CREATIVE	❏ OVERWHELMED	
❏ EXCITED	❏ _____	
❏ _____		

A POSITIVE THOUGHT TO CARRY ME TO SLEEP

_____
_____
_____
_____

MORNING MEDITATION

DATE ___/___/___

TODAY'S FOCUS : _____

_____
_____
_____

AN AFFIRMATION FOR TODAY : _____

_____
_____
_____

WHAT I'GRATEFUL FOR : _____

_____
_____
_____

WHAT I'M EXCITED ABOUT TODAY : _____

_____
_____
_____
_____

HOW I'LL MAKE SPACE FOR GRATITUDE TODAY : ___

_____
_____
_____
_____

MORNING MEDITATION

THINGS I DID TO MAKE A POSITIVE DIFFERENCE TODAY :

_____

_____

_____

_____

❏ HAPPY   ❏ NEUTRAL   NOTES :
❏ CONTENT   ❏ INSECURE   _____
❏ PROUD   ❏ DISOURAGED   _____
❏ HOPEFUL   ❏ DRAINED   _____
❏ LOVING   ❏ SAD   _____
❏ CONNECTED   ❏ SCARED   _____
❏ BALANCED   ❏ ANGRY   _____
❏ JOYFUL   ❏ ANNOYED   _____
❏ RELAXED   ❏ STESSED   _____
❏ CREATIVE   ❏ OVERWHELMED
❏ EXCITED   ❏ _____
❏ _____

A POSITIVE THOUGHT TO CARRY ME TO SLEEP

_____

_____

_____

_____

MORNING MEDITATION

DATE ___/___/___

TODAY'S FOCUS : _____

AN AFFIRMATION FOR TODAY : _____

WHAT I'GRATEFUL FOR : _____

WHAT I'M EXCITED ABOUT TODAY : _____

HOW I'LL MAKE SPACE FOR GRATITUDE TODAY : _____

MORNING MEDITATION

THINGS I DID TO MAKE A POSITIVE DIFFERENCE TODAY :

_____
_____
_____

		NOTES :
❏ HAPPY	❏ NEUTRAL	_____
❏ CONTENT	❏ INSECURE	_____
❏ PROUD	❏ DISOURAGED	_____
❏ HOPEFUL	❏ DRAINED	_____
❏ LOVING	❏ SAD	_____
❏ CONNECTED	❏ SCARED	_____
❏ BALANCED	❏ ANGRY	_____
❏ JOYFUL	❏ ANNOYED	_____
❏ RELAXED	❏ STESSED	_____
❏ CREATIVE	❏ OVERWHELMED	
❏ EXCITED	❏ _____	
❏ _____		

A POSITIVE THOUGHT TO CARRY ME TO SLEEP

_____
_____
_____
_____

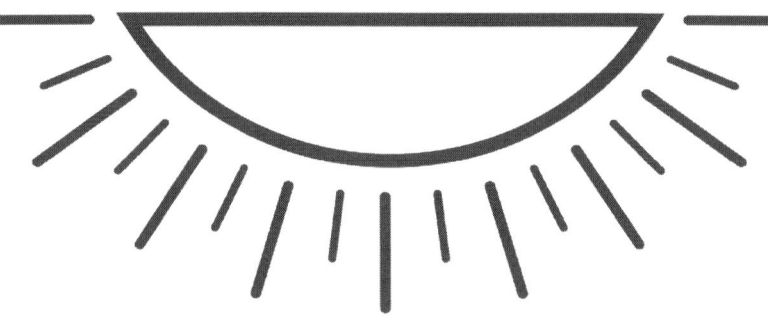

MORNING MEDITATION

DATE __/__/__

TODAY'S FOCUS : _____

AN AFFIRMATION FOR TODAY : _____

WHAT I'GRATEFUL FOR : _____

WHAT I'M EXCITED ABOUT TODAY : _____

HOW I'LL MAKE SPACE FOR GRATITUDE TODAY : _____

MORNING MEDITATION

THINGS I DID TO MAKE A POSITIVE DIFFERENCE TODAY :

_____
_____
_____

❏ HAPPY	❏ NEUTRAL	NOTES :
❏ CONTENT	❏ INSECURE	_____
❏ PROUD	❏ DISOURAGED	_____
❏ HOPEFUL	❏ DRAINED	_____
❏ LOVING	❏ SAD	_____
❏ CONNECTED	❏ SCARED	_____
❏ BALANCED	❏ ANGRY	_____
❏ JOYFUL	❏ ANNOYED	_____
❏ RELAXED	❏ STESSED	_____
❏ CREATIVE	❏ OVERWHELMED	
❏ EXCITED	❏ _____	
❏ _____		

A POSITIVE THOUGHT TO CARRY ME TO SLEEP

_____
_____
_____
_____

MORNING MEDITATION

DATE __/__/__

TODAY'S FOCUS : _____

_____
_____
_____

AN AFFIRMATION FOR TODAY : _____

_____
_____
_____

WHAT I'GRATEFUL FOR : _____

_____
_____
_____

WHAT I'M EXCITED ABOUT TODAY : _____

_____
_____
_____
_____

HOW I'LL MAKE SPACE FOR GRATITUDE TODAY : _____

_____
_____
_____
_____

MORNING MEDITATION

THINGS I DID TO MAKE A POSITIVE DIFFERENCE TODAY :

_____
_____
_____
_____

❏ HAPPY	❏ NEUTRAL	NOTES :
❏ CONTENT	❏ INSECURE	_____
❏ PROUD	❏ DISOURAGED	_____
❏ HOPEFUL	❏ DRAINED	_____
❏ LOVING	❏ SAD	_____
❏ CONNECTED	❏ SCARED	_____
❏ BALANCED	❏ ANGRY	_____
❏ JOYFUL	❏ ANNOYED	_____
❏ RELAXED	❏ STESSED	_____
❏ CREATIVE	❏ OVERWHELMED	
❏ EXCITED	❏ _____	
❏ _____		

A POSITIVE THOUGHT TO CARRY ME TO SLEEP

_____
_____
_____
_____
_____

MORNING MEDITATION

DATE __/__/__

TODAY'S FOCUS :

AN AFFIRMATION FOR TODAY :

WHAT I'GRATEFUL FOR :

WHAT I'M EXCITED ABOUT TODAY :

HOW I'LL MAKE SPACE FOR GRATITUDE TODAY :

MORNING MEDITATION

THINGS I DID TO MAKE A POSITIVE DIFFERENCE TODAY :

- ❏ HAPPY
- ❏ CONTENT
- ❏ PROUD
- ❏ HOPEFUL
- ❏ LOVING
- ❏ CONNECTED
- ❏ BALANCED
- ❏ JOYFUL
- ❏ RELAXED
- ❏ CREATIVE
- ❏ EXCITED
- ❏ _____

- ❏ NEUTRAL
- ❏ INSECURE
- ❏ DISOURAGED
- ❏ DRAINED
- ❏ SAD
- ❏ SCARED
- ❏ ANGRY
- ❏ ANNOYED
- ❏ STESSED
- ❏ OVERWHELMED
- ❏ _____

NOTES :

_____
_____
_____
_____
_____
_____
_____
_____

A POSITIVE THOUGHT TO CARRY ME TO SLEEP

MORNING MEDITATION

DATE ___/___/___

TODAY'S FOCUS :

AN AFFIRMATION FOR TODAY :

WHAT I'GRATEFUL FOR :

WHAT I'M EXCITED ABOUT TODAY :

HOW I'LL MAKE SPACE FOR GRATITUDE TODAY :

MORNING MEDITATION

THINGS I DID TO MAKE A POSITIVE DIFFERENCE TODAY :

_____
_____
_____

❏ HAPPY	❏ NEUTRAL	NOTES :
❏ CONTENT	❏ INSECURE	_____
❏ PROUD	❏ DISOURAGED	_____
❏ HOPEFUL	❏ DRAINED	_____
❏ LOVING	❏ SAD	_____
❏ CONNECTED	❏ SCARED	_____
❏ BALANCED	❏ ANGRY	_____
❏ JOYFUL	❏ ANNOYED	_____
❏ RELAXED	❏ STESSED	_____
❏ CREATIVE	❏ OVERWHELMED	
❏ EXCITED	❏ _____	
❏ _____		

A POSITIVE THOUGHT TO CARRY ME TO SLEEP

_____
_____
_____
_____

With all my Thanks

MORNING MEDITATION

DATE __/__/__

TODAY'S FOCUS : _____

_____
_____
_____

AN AFFIRMATION FOR TODAY : _____

_____
_____

WHAT I'GRATEFUL FOR : _____

_____
_____

WHAT I'M EXCITED ABOUT TODAY : _____

_____
_____
_____

HOW I'LL MAKE SPACE FOR GRATITUDE TODAY : _____

_____
_____
_____

MORNING MEDITATION

THINGS I DID TO MAKE A POSITIVE DIFFERENCE TODAY :

_____
_____
_____

❏ HAPPY	❏ NEUTRAL	NOTES :
❏ CONTENT	❏ INSECURE	_____
❏ PROUD	❏ DISOURAGED	_____
❏ HOPEFUL	❏ DRAINED	_____
❏ LOVING	❏ SAD	_____
❏ CONNECTED	❏ SCARED	_____
❏ BALANCED	❏ ANGRY	_____
❏ JOYFUL	❏ ANNOYED	_____
❏ RELAXED	❏ STESSED	_____
❏ CREATIVE	❏ OVERWHELMED	
❏ EXCITED	❏ _____	
❏ _____		

A POSITIVE THOUGHT TO CARRY ME TO SLEEP

_____
_____
_____
_____

MORNING MEDITATION

DATE __/__/__

TODAY'S FOCUS : _____

_____
_____
_____

AN AFFIRMATION FOR TODAY : _____

_____
_____

WHAT I'GRATEFUL FOR : _____

_____
_____

WHAT I'M EXCITED ABOUT TODAY : _____

_____
_____
_____

HOW I'LL MAKE SPACE FOR GRATITUDE TODAY : _____

_____
_____
_____

MORNING MEDITATION

THINGS I DID TO MAKE A POSITIVE DIFFERENCE TODAY :

_____
_____
_____

❏ HAPPY	❏ NEUTRAL	NOTES :
❏ CONTENT	❏ INSECURE	_____
❏ PROUD	❏ DISOURAGED	_____
❏ HOPEFUL	❏ DRAINED	_____
❏ LOVING	❏ SAD	_____
❏ CONNECTED	❏ SCARED	_____
❏ BALANCED	❏ ANGRY	_____
❏ JOYFUL	❏ ANNOYED	_____
❏ RELAXED	❏ STESSED	_____
❏ CREATIVE	❏ OVERWHELMED	
❏ EXCITED	❏ _____	
❏ _____		

A POSITIVE THOUGHT TO CARRY ME TO SLEEP

_____
_____
_____
_____

MORNING MEDITATION

DATE __ / __ / __

TODAY'S FOCUS : _____

AN AFFIRMATION FOR TODAY : _____

WHAT I'GRATEFUL FOR : _____

WHAT I'M EXCITED ABOUT TODAY : _____

HOW I'LL MAKE SPACE FOR GRATITUDE TODAY : _____

MORNING MEDITATION

THINGS I DID TO MAKE A POSITIVE DIFFERENCE TODAY :

_____

_____

_____

- ❏ HAPPY
- ❏ CONTENT
- ❏ PROUD
- ❏ HOPEFUL
- ❏ LOVING
- ❏ CONNECTED
- ❏ BALANCED
- ❏ JOYFUL
- ❏ RELAXED
- ❏ CREATIVE
- ❏ EXCITED
- ❏ _____

- ❏ NEUTRAL
- ❏ INSECURE
- ❏ DISOURAGED
- ❏ DRAINED
- ❏ SAD
- ❏ SCARED
- ❏ ANGRY
- ❏ ANNOYED
- ❏ STESSED
- ❏ OVERWHELMED
- ❏ _____

NOTES :

_____
_____
_____
_____
_____
_____
_____
_____

A POSITIVE THOUGHT TO CARRY ME TO SLEEP

_____

_____

_____

_____

MORNING MEDITATION

DATE ___/___/___

TODAY'S FOCUS :

AN AFFIRMATION FOR TODAY :

WHAT I'GRATEFUL FOR :

WHAT I'M EXCITED ABOUT TODAY :

HOW I'LL MAKE SPACE FOR GRATITUDE TODAY :

MORNING MEDITATION

THINGS I DID TO MAKE A POSITIVE DIFFERENCE TODAY :

_____
_____
_____

❏ HAPPY	❏ NEUTRAL	NOTES :
❏ CONTENT	❏ INSECURE	_____
❏ PROUD	❏ DISOURAGED	_____
❏ HOPEFUL	❏ DRAINED	_____
❏ LOVING	❏ SAD	_____
❏ CONNECTED	❏ SCARED	_____
❏ BALANCED	❏ ANGRY	_____
❏ JOYFUL	❏ ANNOYED	_____
❏ RELAXED	❏ STESSED	_____
❏ CREATIVE	❏ OVERWHELMED	
❏ EXCITED	❏ _____	
❏ _____		

A POSITIVE THOUGHT TO CARRY ME TO SLEEP

_____
_____
_____
_____

MORNING MEDITATION

DATE ___/___/___

TODAY'S FOCUS : _____

_____
_____
_____

AN AFFIRMATION FOR TODAY : _____

_____
_____

WHAT I'GRATEFUL FOR : _____

_____
_____
_____

WHAT I'M EXCITED ABOUT TODAY : _____

_____
_____
_____

HOW I'LL MAKE SPACE FOR GRATITUDE TODAY : _____

_____
_____
_____

MORNING MEDITATION

THINGS I DID TO MAKE A POSITIVE DIFFERENCE TODAY :

_____

_____

_____

❏ HAPPY	❏ NEUTRAL	NOTES :
❏ CONTENT	❏ INSECURE	_____
❏ PROUD	❏ DISOURAGED	_____
❏ HOPEFUL	❏ DRAINED	_____
❏ LOVING	❏ SAD	_____
❏ CONNECTED	❏ SCARED	_____
❏ BALANCED	❏ ANGRY	_____
❏ JOYFUL	❏ ANNOYED	_____
❏ RELAXED	❏ STESSED	_____
❏ CREATIVE	❏ OVERWHELMED	
❏ EXCITED	❏ _____	
❏ _____		

A POSITIVE THOUGHT TO CARRY ME TO SLEEP

_____

_____

_____

_____

Many Thanks

MORNING MEDITATION

DATE ___/___/___

TODAY'S FOCUS : _____

AN AFFIRMATION FOR TODAY : _____

WHAT I'GRATEFUL FOR : _____

WHAT I'M EXCITED ABOUT TODAY : _____

HOW I'LL MAKE SPACE FOR GRATITUDE TODAY : _____

MORNING MEDITATION

THINGS I DID TO MAKE A POSITIVE DIFFERENCE TODAY :

_____
_____
_____

- ❏ HAPPY
- ❏ CONTENT
- ❏ PROUD
- ❏ HOPEFUL
- ❏ LOVING
- ❏ CONNECTED
- ❏ BALANCED
- ❏ JOYFUL
- ❏ RELAXED
- ❏ CREATIVE
- ❏ EXCITED
- ❏ _____

- ❏ NEUTRAL
- ❏ INSECURE
- ❏ DISOURAGED
- ❏ DRAINED
- ❏ SAD
- ❏ SCARED
- ❏ ANGRY
- ❏ ANNOYED
- ❏ STESSED
- ❏ OVERWHELMED
- ❏ _____

NOTES :
_____
_____
_____
_____
_____
_____
_____
_____

A POSITIVE THOUGHT TO CARRY ME TO SLEEP

_____
_____
_____
_____

MORNING MEDITATION

DATE __/__/__

TODAY'S FOCUS :

AN AFFIRMATION FOR TODAY :

WHAT I'GRATEFUL FOR :

WHAT I'M EXCITED ABOUT TODAY :

HOW I'LL MAKE SPACE FOR GRATITUDE TODAY :

MORNING MEDITATION

THINGS I DID TO MAKE A POSITIVE DIFFERENCE TODAY :

❏ HAPPY	❏ NEUTRAL	NOTES :
❏ CONTENT	❏ INSECURE	
❏ PROUD	❏ DISOURAGED	
❏ HOPEFUL	❏ DRAINED	
❏ LOVING	❏ SAD	
❏ CONNECTED	❏ SCARED	
❏ BALANCED	❏ ANGRY	
❏ JOYFUL	❏ ANNOYED	
❏ RELAXED	❏ STESSED	
❏ CREATIVE	❏ OVERWHELMED	
❏ EXCITED	❏ _____	
❏ _____		

A POSITIVE THOUGHT TO CARRY ME TO SLEEP

MORNING MEDITATION

DATE ___/___/___

TODAY'S FOCUS : _____

_____
_____
_____

AN AFFIRMATION FOR TODAY : _____

_____
_____
_____

WHAT I'GRATEFUL FOR : _____

_____
_____
_____

WHAT I'M EXCITED ABOUT TODAY : _____

_____
_____
_____

HOW I'LL MAKE SPACE FOR GRATITUDE TODAY : _____

_____
_____
_____

MORNING MEDITATION

THINGS I DID TO MAKE A POSITIVE DIFFERENCE TODAY :

_____
_____
_____

- ❏ HAPPY
- ❏ CONTENT
- ❏ PROUD
- ❏ HOPEFUL
- ❏ LOVING
- ❏ CONNECTED
- ❏ BALANCED
- ❏ JOYFUL
- ❏ RELAXED
- ❏ CREATIVE
- ❏ EXCITED
- ❏ _____

- ❏ NEUTRAL
- ❏ INSECURE
- ❏ DISOURAGED
- ❏ DRAINED
- ❏ SAD
- ❏ SCARED
- ❏ ANGRY
- ❏ ANNOYED
- ❏ STESSED
- ❏ OVERWHELMED
- ❏ _____

NOTES :

_____
_____
_____
_____
_____
_____
_____
_____
_____

A POSITIVE THOUGHT TO CARRY ME TO SLEEP

_____
_____
_____
_____

MORNING MEDITATION

DATE __/__/__

TODAY'S FOCUS : _____

AN AFFIRMATION FOR TODAY : _____

WHAT I'GRATEFUL FOR : _____

WHAT I'M EXCITED ABOUT TODAY : _____

HOW I'LL MAKE SPACE FOR GRATITUDE TODAY : _____

MORNING MEDITATION

THINGS I DID TO MAKE A POSITIVE DIFFERENCE TODAY :

- ❏ HAPPY
- ❏ CONTENT
- ❏ PROUD
- ❏ HOPEFUL
- ❏ LOVING
- ❏ CONNECTED
- ❏ BALANCED
- ❏ JOYFUL
- ❏ RELAXED
- ❏ CREATIVE
- ❏ EXCITED
- ❏ _____

- ❏ NEUTRAL
- ❏ INSECURE
- ❏ DISOURAGED
- ❏ DRAINED
- ❏ SAD
- ❏ SCARED
- ❏ ANGRY
- ❏ ANNOYED
- ❏ STESSED
- ❏ OVERWHELMED
- ❏ _____

NOTES :
___
___
___
___
___
___
___
___

A POSITIVE THOUGHT TO CARRY ME TO SLEEP

MORNING MEDITATION

DATE __/__/__

TODAY'S FOCUS : _____

_____
_____
_____

AN AFFIRMATION FOR TODAY : _____

_____
_____

WHAT I'GRATEFUL FOR : _____

_____
_____

WHAT I'M EXCITED ABOUT TODAY : _____

_____
_____
_____

HOW I'LL MAKE SPACE FOR GRATITUDE TODAY : _____

_____
_____
_____

MORNING MEDITATION

THINGS I DID TO MAKE A POSITIVE DIFFERENCE TODAY :

_____
_____
_____

❑ HAPPY	❑ NEUTRAL	NOTES :
❑ CONTENT	❑ INSECURE	_____
❑ PROUD	❑ DISOURAGED	_____
❑ HOPEFUL	❑ DRAINED	_____
❑ LOVING	❑ SAD	_____
❑ CONNECTED	❑ SCARED	_____
❑ BALANCED	❑ ANGRY	_____
❑ JOYFUL	❑ ANNOYED	_____
❑ RELAXED	❑ STESSED	_____
❑ CREATIVE	❑ OVERWHELMED	
❑ EXCITED	❑ _____	
❑ _____		

A POSITIVE THOUGHT TO CARRY ME TO SLEEP

_____
_____
_____
_____

Many Thanks